NETAJI

Krishna Bose is an eminent writer, educationist and parliamentarian.

She has been a three time member of Parliament in India in the 11th, 12th and 13th Lok Sabhas. During the term of the 13th Lok Sabha she served as chairperson of the Parliamentary Standing Committee on External Affairs in India which oversees the conduct of India's foreign policy.

Krishna Bose was the head of the Department of English and later the principal of City College (South) of Calcutta. She is a leading contemporary writer of Calcutta with many books and articles. Her latest book is her memoir *An Outsider in Politics* (Penguin Books). Her other books include *Itihaser Sandhane* (Ananda Publishers), *Charanarekha Taba* (Ananda Publishers), *Prasanga Subhas Chandra* (Ananda Publishers), *Smriti-Bismriti* (Ananda Publishers), *Ek Nambar Bari* (Ananda Publishers), *Je Taranikhani* (Ananda Publishers), and *Parliament-er Andarmahale* (Ananda Publishers).

Actively involved in public work, Krishna Bose is the chairperson of Netaji Research Bureau, an institution of history, politics and current affairs, president of the Institute of Child Health, Calcutta, chairperson of Centre of Archaeological Studies & Training, Eastern India, and president of Vivek Chetana—an organization for disadvantaged women and children. She has been a member of PEN and has served as an executive committee member for a long time. At present, she is vice chairperson of PEN, West Bengal.

NETAJI
A Biography for the Young

Krishna Bose

First published in 1995 by
Rupa Publications India Pvt. Ltd.
7/16, Ansari Road, Daryaganj
New Delhi 110002

Sales centres:
Prayagraj Bengaluru Chennai
Hyderabad Jaipur Kathmandu
Kolkata Mumbai

Copyright © Krishna Bose 1995

The views and opinions expressed in this book are the author's own and the facts are as reported by him, which have been verified to the extent possible, and the publishers are not in any way liable for the same. Names of some people have been changed to protect their privacy.

All rights reserved.
No part of this publication may be reproduced, transmitted, or stored in a retrieval system, in any form or by any means, electronic, mechanical, photocopying, recording or otherwise, without the prior permission of the publisher.

P-ISBN: 978-81-716-7279-0
E-ISBN: 978-81-291-2250-6

Sixteenth impression 2023

20 19 18 17 16

The moral right of the author has been asserted.

Typeset by Nikita Overseas Pvt. Ltd. New Delhi

Printed in India

This book is sold subject to the condition that it shall not, by way of trade or otherwise, be lent, resold, hired out, or otherwise circulated, without the publisher's prior consent, in any form of binding or cover other than that in which it is published.

For
Peter Arun, Thomas Krishna, Maya Karina

Contents

I.	The Great Escape	1
II.	Growing Up	10
III.	The Freedom Fighter	20
IV.	Rashtrapati and After	32
V.	Azad Hind	41
VI.	A Perilous Journey	47
VII.	Onto Delhi	51
VIII.	Victory in Defeat	59

I

THE GREAT ESCAPE

It was a cold winter night in Calcutta in January 1941. In the dim moonlight a three-storeyed house in Elgin Road looked quiet and sleepy. A light, however, burnt in the north-east room on the first floor. A few yards away from the gate of the house three or four men were getting ready to settle down in their beds spread on wooden charpoys. They were no ordinary pavement dwellers. In fact, they were plainclothes policemen who kept a sharp watch on the Elgin Road house.

The man who lived in the lighted up bedroom on the first floor was known to be a dangerous person to the British who ruled India at that time. But the guards knew he was too ill to move out of his room. So they only kept an eye on the people who came to see him. On that night they yawned sleepily and drew their blankets over their heads and fell asleep.

drew their blankets over their heads and fell asleep.

It was already past midnight. The clock moved on. At half past one a car came out of the house. There was nothing suspicious about it. It came out in the most normal fashion, turned south and drove onwards. The policemen could never imagine that in that car was the man for whom they were keeping a night-and-day vigil on the house. The light in the bedroom still burnt innocently and the guards slept peacefully on their hard wooden beds.

The man who escaped from that house that night was none other than Netaji Subhas Chandra Bose, the great leader and patriot.

At the end of 1939, World War II broke out and Britain was locked in a fierce battle with Germany. Netaji thought that this was the opportunity to strike hard at the British Raj. But time went by. And at the end of 1940, Subhas Chandra Bose was in prison. So he undertook a fast unto death and gave an ultimatum to the British Government—'Release me or I shall refuse to live.' The British Government did not wish to take any chances. So they promptly released him, although secretly they decided that as soon as he would be a little better they would arrest him again. But Netaji had other plans. One of the most daring escapes in history took the British Government completely by surprise and when they woke up to it, Netaji had crossed the Indian border and entered Afghanistan.

The car which went out of the Elgin Road house was going southwards only to mislead the police. Soon it changed direction and proceeded northwards. The sleepy city of Calcutta was left behind and the car sped along the Grand Trunk Road.

Netaji sat in the back seat dressed like an upcountry

Muslim in a long coat and pajamas complete with a fez cap. He called himself Mohammad Ziauddin, an insurance agent. His suitcase bore the initials M.Z. A young man dressed in the usual Bengali manner in a dhoti and a coat but with a Kashmiri cap on his head was driving the car. This was Netaji's nephew, a young medical student, and his name was Sisir.

As they drove on, Netaji now and then poured coffee from a flask and held it for his nephew to drink. Now and then he exchanged a few words with Sisir. Both of them had to keep wide awake and be alert. Netaji asked him, 'Do you know the story of the Irish hero De Valera's escape from prison?' Well, he did know the story. Netaji was remembering the other great political escapes on that fateful night.

Although there were a few anxious moments, the drive through the night was on the whole safe. Once the car had to stop at a railway crossing for quite some time. The sleepy gateman delayed opening the gate. Another time Sisir had to apply the brakes suddenly when the car was about to collide with a pack of buffaloes crossing the road. The frightened animals jostled against the car.

Morning brought them to a small colliery township called Bararee near Dhanbad. Netaji could not travel in the daytime. He was so well known someone might recognize him. So for the day he took shelter in the bungalow of Asoke, another nephew of his. At night the journey was resumed and Netaji was driven to the Gomoh station. He bade goodbye and climbed up the steps of the overbridge and disappeared on the other side. The Delhi-Kalka Mail arrived and left the station. His companions heard the train steam off and then saw a garland of lights moving away and away to the tune of rhytiimic clatter of the moving wheels.

After a change of trains in Delhi, Netaji arrived at the Peshawar Cantonment station. The man in charge of Netaji's escape plan at the Peshawar end was his close political associate, Mian Akbar Shah. Akbar Shah had planned everything but the man who actually accompanied Netaji from Peshawar to Kabul was Bhagat Ram Talwar.

Bhagat Ram took the pseudonym Rahamat Khan. On January 26th, Rahamat Khan and Netaji set out on a perilous journey. A car dropped them at the border of the tribal area from where they started their trek on foot. The first night they spent inside a mosque in a small village.

Next day, early in the morning, he had breakfast with parathas and tea and then started to trek. By midday they reached a village and hired a mule for Netaji. The mule ride was on the whole, quite comfortable. But once, while going downhill, he fell from the mule. Fortunately, he was not hurt much.

Late in the night, they reached a village. The muleman took them to a villager's house. The villager lived in a one-room hut. He had got married on that very day. His bride was sleeping on a cot and there were a number of goats in another corner of the room. The man woke up his bride who happily cooked scrambled eggs and parathas for her unknown guests. Netaji was very hungry. He enjoyed his dinner. There was no time to rest. Their host said they should complete the journey before daybreak. So off they went again.

Netaji was pretending to be deaf and dumb because he did not know the local language. He was supposed to be Rahamat Khan's uncle and as he was ill, Rahamat Khan was taking him to a shrine called Adda Sharif. Netaji acted the part of a deaf and dumb person very well. That day, a Pathan villager accosted them on the road and asked them all sorts of questions. He insisted on examining Netaji's tongue. So Netaji put out his tongue and held it very stiff. The man poked his tongue with his fingers and said, indeed, something was wrong with it and even suggested a treatment with solution of alum and hot water.

Netaji and Rahamat Khan spent two nights at Jalalabad. From Jalalabad they went to offer prayers at Adda Sharif and also visited a tribal chief, Haji Mohammed Amin, who helped revolutionaries and lived at a village called Lalmon. He gave them helpful tips for the rest of the journey.

Next day, Netaji and Rahamat Khan continued their journey partly by tonga, partly on trucks loaded with tea chests, and partly on foot. On January 29th, they reached the city of Kabul. As they sat in an ordinary sarm near Lahori Gate, Netaji heard—by chance—the radio news which announced Subhas Chandra Bose had disappeared from his Calcutta home. Ten days after his actual disappearance, the British police came to know about it on January 27th.

Reaching Kabul was only part of Netaji's journey. He now needed help to get out of Afghanistan. If he was arrested in Kabul, the Afghan Government might have to hand him over to the British. So Netaji and Rahamat Khan tried to contact the foreign embassies in Kabul for help.

In the meantime, an Afghan policeman became very suspicious. He started visiting them at the *sarai* and continuously demanded money. One day he demanded Netaji's wristwatch and he had to part with it. Netaji also fell ill at the *sarai*. Rahamat Khan had contacted the Russian embassy but they did not respond. It was a most difficult time for Netaji.

There was an Indian in Kabul at that time who owned a shop. His name was Uttamchand. Rahamat Khan took him into confidence. Uttamchand took Netaji into his house. He and his wife looked after him with great devotion.

In the meantime, contact had been established with the German and Italian legations. They were making arrangements for Netaji's travel to Berlin. He had to go via Moscow for which a Russian visa was necessary. Another long wait ensued. The wife of the Italian envoy, Mrs. Quaroni, served as the go-between. She used to come to Uttamchand's shop pretending to buy something and passed on whatever news there was. Netaji was becoming restless. He was stuck in Kabul for forty-five days.

At last good news arrived. All arrangements were ready. Netaji moved to the German legation. There was an Italian officer at the Italian legation whose name was Orlando Mazzotta. Netaji's photograph was put in his passport. Netaji bade goodbye to Uttamchand, his wife and Rahamat Khan and disguised as Orlando Mazzotta left Kabul with two other German officers in a car. After crossing the frontier he travelled by train to Moscow. From there he flew to Berlin.

Subhas Chandra Bose was not heard of for a year. Then the whole world was startled one day to hear a powerful voice over the radio proclaim: 'This is Subhas Chandra Bose speaking to you over the Azad Hind Radio.'

II
GROWING UP

The house from which Subhas Chandra Bose escaped on January 17th, 1941, is now Calcutta's Netaji Museum. In the first room of the museum there is a page from the diary of Janakinath Bose. 'A boy was born at midday'—is the entry on the page dated January 23rd, 1897. Yes, Subhas was born in Cuttack on January 23rd, 1897. He was the ninth child of Janakinath and Prabhabati. Janakinath Bose was a well-established lawyer of Cuttack at that time. And Prabhabati was a woman of personality. A strict mother to all her fourteen children.

At the age of five, Subhas started going to school. On the first day he was so excited that as he ran to the coach which was to take him to school, he had a fall and had to stay back. He was disappointed. It was perhaps a pointer to the turbulent life which awaited him in the years to come.

Little Subhas did not know a single word of English when he started going to Cuttack's fashionable English-medium school. He and his uncle, who was his classmate, were sharpening pencils one day. Subhas thought he had sharpened his much better than his uncle Ranendra had done his. So he declared, '—Ranendra mot, I shor' (in Bengali *mota* is fat and *shorn* thin) and thought he spoke wonderful English. However, he was intelligent and hardworking and soon he topped his class. He was always good at studies but not so good at games.

There was a change of his school at the age twelve. Subhas got transferred to the Ravenshaw Collegiate School. If English was his problem at the missionary school, Bengali posed a bigger problem in the new school. In the seven years that he spent at the Anglo-Indian school he was never taught Bengali. So at the new school the first time he wrote an essay on a cow, or was it a horse? he made ridiculous mistakes. The teacher read aloud his composition and the boys tittered. Subhas felt humiliated but accepted the challenge. Quietly he started studying Bengali. It was a struggle for weeks and months. And lo! at the annual examination who comes first in Bengali? It was none other than Subhas Chandra Bose.

The man who influenced him very much in his schooldays was his Headmaster, Benimadhab Das. From him he learnt to appreciate the beauty of nature. But what is more important, he infused in Subhas a sense of moral values. He learnt to distinguish what is right from what is wrong.

But it was Swami Vivekananda's writings which influenced him most in his boyhood days. Just when he was groping for an ideal in life he accidentally came across the works of

12

Vivekananda at a relative's house. He borrowed the books and read them hungrily. The words of Vivekananda—'Say brothers, at the top of your voice—the naked Indian, the illiterate Indian, the Brahmin Indian, the pariah Indian is my brother'—kept ringing in his ears. Service to mankind, Subhas realized, included service to his country. Service to mankind and your own salvation—was his ideal from that time.

Young Subhas devoted himself to social work. He was neglecting his studies which his parents disapproved of. Subhas felt sorry he was causing anxiety to his parents, but felt helpless. He had to do what his conscience dictated.

To his mother he wrote at this time: 'Mother, what sort of career for us will please you most?... I do not know if you will be the happiest if we grow up to be judges, magistrates, barristers or high-placed officials ... or if we earn the respect of the learned and the virtuous for having grown up to be 'real men' even though we may be poor. I am most anxious to know what you would most like your son to be.'

On the other hand, a religious side was opening up in his character. He was practising meditation and yoga. He poured his heart out in long philosophic letters to his mother. He realized that as all rivers flow to the ocean all our lives flow towards God.

Despite all sorts of distractions, Subhas passed the entrance or school leaving examination with flying colours. He ranked second in the University examination which made his parents very happy indeed.

Subhas came to Calcutta to study at the Presidency College. His college career turned out to be very exciting and eventful. He began on a quiet note, taking interest in extra-curricular activities. He arranged debates, relief funds for flood and famine. He used to walk back to his Elgin Road home from college, a distance of about three miles. The money thus saved he gave to an old beggar woman who sat on the pavement near his home.

The religious urge was still in him. One day, he left home along with a friend in search of a guru. He went from place to place in North India. He visited pilgrimages like Hardwar, Varanasi, Agra, Mathura and Brindaban. It was a great experience for him. Just as he met many deeply religious persons who were worth meeting, he also became aware of some of the not so good things of our religion. Even monks who preached all men to be children of God, in practice would not let them sit and eat at the same place with higher caste people. They were not allowed to draw water from a well because they were not Brahmins.

All this disillusioned him. Besides, some of the really honest and good sadhus asked him to go back. This was not his way of life, he was told. In the meantime, in Calcutta, his parents were distraught with anxiety and were looking for him. An astrologer said Subhas was in a place the name of which began with a 'B'. His family thought B could mean Baidyanath. So someone was sent to Deoghar in Santhal Parganas, where there was the temple of Baidyanath, in search for him. But as a matter of fact he was then at Varanasi which at that time was known as Banaras.

To the relief of everybody, one fine morning Subhas was back home. His father received him with his usual calm and dignity. His mother wept and said he would be the cause of her death! As a result of this adventure Subhas fell ill with typhoid fever.

This was the end of one adventure but the next one that overtook him in college was of a more serious nature and proved to be a turning point in his life.

Subhas was studying in the third year class at Presidency College. Professor Oaten, an English professor, misbehaved with Indian students. The students felt insulted. There was a strike in the college. The incident was somehow patched up by the authorities. But after some time the same professor again insulted an Indian student. The students decided to teach him a lesson. The professor was beaten up in the college corridor.

Indian students beating up an English professor was a sensational thing at that time. Subhas was expelled from the college as he was a well-known leader of the students.

'Do you support the beating up of your professor?'—he was asked by the enquiry commission. Subhas replied that there was grave provocation for it. Whether he really took part in the actual beating or not was not known for certain at that time. Asked about it by friends he only smiled. But what is most interesting is this that Professor Oaten in his old age wrote a beautiful poem on his student Subhas where he paid tribute to his patriotism. He said: 'Did I once suffer, Subhas, at your hand? Your patriot heart is stilled! I would forget!'

About this incident many years later Subhas said that it was the first time he felt the glory of leadership and also experienced the sacrifice which went with it.

'My principal expelled me but he also decided the course of my future life,' Subhas said.

After a year of punishment, Subhas was allowed to resume his studies at the Scottish Church College of Calcutta. Subhas got his first military training at about this time. There was a

University training corps which he joined. He enjoyed rifle shooting practices and learnt a lot from a four-month military camp life. The officers of the corps had no idea that they were training the future Commander-in-Chief of the Azad Hind Fauj.

Subhas did not, however, neglect his studies any more. In the B.A. examination he ranked first class second in philosophy.

Subhas decided that he would take up psychology for his M.A. studies. Years afterwards he wrote to a friend that if he had not gone into politics he would have become a psychologist. But destiny had planned a different sort of life for him. His father called him one day. He found his second brother Sarat also present in the room. He was asked if he would like to go to England and sit for the I.C.S. examination. In those days to become an I.C.S. officer was a great thing. The life of an I.C.S. officer was a life of wealth, power and comfort. But it meant you became a government servant. Subhas would have to serve the British Government who ruled over India. There was a conflict in Subhas's mind. He was given only twenty-four hours to make up his mind.

He decided he would go. He wanted to go abroad to gather experience of the outer world. Whether or not to be an I.C.S. officer he could decide later. He may not even pass the I.C.S. examination, who knows?—he thought. The examination was very tough and he would get only eight months to prepare.

The ship 'City of Calcutta' brought him to England in September 1919. He got admission into Cambridge University and studied mental and moral science for his Tripos. Preparation for the I.C.S. examination also went on.

In July 1920, he sat for the exam. He felt that he was not well prepared and he knew competition would be tough. So after the examination was over he wrote to his people in Calcutta that he had not done well and could not expect to be selected.

He was greatly surprised therefore, when he found that he had not only passed the I.C.S. examination but had come fourth in the list. He was happy and sent a telegram to his family.

But now he was faced with a very difficult situation. He wanted to dedicate his life for national service. He was certain he could serve his country much better if he was one of the people and not a member of a foreign government. On the other hand, he knew he would cause deep pain and displeasure to his father and mother if he gave up such a promising career. He wrote long letters to his elder brother Sarat explaining his mental condition and asking him to put in a word to his father. He also wrote to Deshbandhu C.R. Das offering his services to the nation. Sarat always looked upon this younger brother of his with indulgence and sympathy. He seemed to have realized very early the latent genius of the young man. Subhas also looked up to him for guidance whenever he was faced with a crisis. He knew many would criticize his decision to give up the I.C.S. But he appealed to Sarat.

'I am sure many of our relatives will howl when they hear of such a rash and dangerous proposal.... But I do not care for their opinions, their cheers or their taunts. But I have faith in your idealism and that is why I am appealing to you.' He reminded his elder brother of the moral support he gave him when he was expelled from Presidency College. He also clearly stated the kind of life he wanted to live. 'A life of sacrifice to start with, plain living and high thinking, wholehearted devotion to the country's cause—all these are highly enchanting to my imagination and inclination.'

On April 22nd, 1921, Subhas Chandra Bose sent in his resignation from the I.C.S. On that very day, in a letter to one of his childhood friends, he wrote that his inner voice was telling him that he would never find happiness in power, property or wealth. The way to happiness, according to him, lay in dancing around with the surging waves of the ocean.

III
THE FREEDOM FIGHTER

It was the month of July, 1921. Subhas Chandra Bose came back to India. He travelled in the same ship with Rabindranath Tagore. Subhas Chandra had already become quite well known after his resignation from the I.C.S. At that time, Gandhiji had given the call for a non-cooperation movement in India, that is, he had called upon his countrymen not to cooperate with the British Government in any way. He had called upon the students to leave schools and colleges. He had urged government employees to leave their jobs and to join the national movement. There was overwhelming response from the people. Young Bose and the poet discussed the situation at home during their voyage. Tagore had reservations about the boycott of educational institutions. He advocated more constructive work. Subhas was, however, full of enthusiasm for the non-cooperation movement.

As soon as he landed in Bombay, Subhas went to meet Mahatma Gandhi who was in Bombay at that time. They had a long talk on the prospects of the non-cooperation movement and on Gandhiji's cult of non-violence. Subhas had many questions to ask. Gandhiji explained his point of view to the young man patiently. At a time when the whole of India was under the spell of Gandhiji it was significant that Subhas Chandra Bose dared to ask him questions and clarifications and even expressed his own opinion freely. Subhas Chandra Bose realized there was a difference of approach between the two but he did work closely under Gandhiji in the Indian National Congress from 1921 to 1939.

In that first meeting, Gandhiji advised him to go to Deshbandhu C.R. Das in Calcutta. C.R. Das was a big barrister but he had given up his lucrative practice and comfortable way of life in order to serve his motherland. His countrymen affectionately called him 'Deshbandhu'. Subhas Chandra had already written to him from Cambridge and told him that he had given up the I.C.S. and wished to dedicate himself to the service of the nation. The meeting between Deshbandhu and Subhas Chandra was very touching. Subhas found his political guru and Deshbandhu found a loyal lieutenant in him.

Subhas Chandra started work as the principal of the National College. The National College had been established for students who had given up education at the government institutions. At first there was a rush of students but later not many students could be found for the college. But Subhas was very serious about his new job. He would sit in the empty class and look through papers and files. There is a well-known joke about him. Somebody came to the college and asked, 'Where is Subhas Babu?' One of his colleagues replied, 'Ah, Subhas? He is in the class teaching empty benches!'

Subhas had his first taste of organizing a large-scale agitation against the government at the time of the visit of the Prince of Wales. The Indian people decided to boycott the visit of the British prince in order to show their disapproval of the British Raj. The day the Prince of Wales arrived in India there was complete hartal (strike) throughout the country. In Calcutta, Subhas was in charge of the Congress volunteers. After the strike the government declared the volunteers unlawful. And a call for Satyagraha was given. Many people courted arrest. Basanti Devi, wife of Deshbandhu, also courted arrest by hawking khadi. She was soon released but both Deshbandhu Das and Subhas Chandra Bose were imprisoned

at this time. When Subhas was told at the court that he was being imprisoned for six months, he was rather disappointed. 'Only six months?' he asked. 'Have I stolen a fowl?' It was, however, only the beginning. Soon, his life was to become a chain of imprisonments and exile.

During this first imprisonment, Deshbandhu and Subhas Chandra were in the same prison. Subhas used to look after Deshbandhu. He often prepared his meals, fried puri and bhaji for him. Deshbandhu's friends and fellow prisoners jokingly said, 'So, Deshbandhu has an I.C.S. for a cook.'

Basanti Devi often visited them in prison. There was a tender bond of affection between Basanti Devi and Subhas. Basanti Devi looked upon him as her own son and Subhas called her mother. Basanti Devi used to recount in her old age the greatness of Subhas's own mother who used to tell her, 'You are the real mother, I am only the nurse.'

The twenties were the time of Bose's apprenticeship in various fields of national service. And in whatever field he chose to work, he did so with great distinction. As soon as he was out of prison he organized relief work during the floods in North Bengal. His relief work drew praise even from Lord Lytton. He also had a stint of journalism. He edited political magazines like *Banglar Katha*, *Atmasakti* and *Forward*. He wrote profusely about the different problems facing India. He also turned his attention to the youth and organized the All Bengal Youth League.

At the Gaya Congress session of 1922, Motilal Nehru and Deshbandhu formed a party within the Congress known as Swarajya Party. They were of the opinion that the Congress should take part in the elections and get into the assemblies so that they could fight from within the legislatures as well. Subhas Chandra was an untiring worker of the Swarajya Party. Gandhiji was initially opposed to this policy but later he also came round.

In 1924, the Congress captured the Calcutta Corporation. Deshbandhu was the Mayor and Subhas Chandra became the Chief Executive, a post so long held exclusively by Englishmen. At first Subhas was somewhat hesitant. Did he give up the I.C.S. only to be the chief executive officer of the Calcutta Corporation? But when he plunged into work he did so wholeheartedly. All the different problems of the city of Calcutta claimed his attention—be it clearance of garbage from the streets of Calcutta or beautification of the Strand along the river Hooghly. His administrative ability came to the fore at this time. But alas! it was only for a brief period that he had the opportunity to serve his city.

In October 1924, Subhas Chandra was arrested and sent to prison in Burma. The British in those days loved to send Indian revolutionaries to prison in faraway places like Burma or the Andaman Islands. Subhas felt proud that he was in the same prison where Tilak had served a six-year term and Lala Lajpat Rai had also been imprisoned.

Subhas Chandra always felt restless in prison, restless because imprisonment meant he could not serve his motherland. In Burma, he tried his best to adjust himself to prison life. He shared with other fellow prisoners all the inconveniences. He, however, had a keen sense of humour and wrote home to his sister-in-law—his elder brother Sarat's wife, Bivabati—all the funny anecdotes of prison life.

The political prisoners had selected one amongst them to be the Manager in charge of the kitchen and store. Subhas wrote home that the 'Manager' was serving them good food. One day he even produced rasgullas. But the rasgullas were so hard that if one was thrown at a person it would surely result in a fractured skull.

He also mentioned Shyamlal, an ordinary convict on whom the political prisoners bestowed the title 'Pandit'. His wisdom knew no bounds. He saw that the water meant for the bath of the prisoners was being wasted. So he got into the bathroom and closed the door from inside. Then he jumped out of the window and somehow closed the window shutters too. Now he felt relieved that no one could waste water anymore. Then it was time for bath and the prisoners could not get into the bathroom at all. On that very day he acquired the tide 'Pandit'.

But Subhas's health deteriorated alarmingly in Burmese prison. It was suspected that he even had a touch of tuberculosis. It was in prison that he got the news of the death of Deshbandhu Das, his political guru. It was a great blow to him.

After prolonged argument and struggle, the British Government brought him back to Calcutta in 1927 and released him.

The most important thing for him on release was to recoup his health. He went to the hill resort of Shillong with his parents, his brother Sarat's family and other relatives. He was very fond of his nephews and nieces. He had definite opinions about the education and upbringing of children. Children should read the Ramayana and the Mahabharata in order to understand the heritage of India. Apart from formal education they must learn to draw and to sing. Future India needed accomplished citizens. Subhas loved to play with his nephews and nieces. At Shillong he played hide and seek with them. Soon he regained his health and was his old self.

Subhas Chandra was back in active politics. The Simon

Commission headed by a British peer, Lord Simon, arrived in India in November 1927. The Commission was supposed to suggest reform measures for India. But the Indian people rejected the Commission. 'Simon go back', was the cry everywhere and Subhas Bose was busy organizing boycott of the Simon Commission. At Lahore, Lala Lajpat Rai, the great Indian patriot, received lathi blows on his chest in one demonstration and eventually died.

Subhas Chandra now became, along with Jawaharlal Nehru, general secretary of the Congress. At this time, both Nehru, who was eight years elder to him, and Netaji, emerged as youth leaders and promoters of progressive modern ideas.

Subhas Chandra also became interested in the welfare of the workers. In 1928, he organized a massive strike at Tata's at Jamshedpur. He later became the President of the All India Trade Union Congress.

In 1928, the Congress session was held in Calcutta. Motilal Nehru was the President. Subhas was the General Officer Commanding of the volunteer force. He organized the volunteers with strict military discipline. He himself donned a military uniform and even rode on horseback. Young boys and girls marched in uniform. It was a very impressive show. Perhaps the seed of the future Chief of State and Army Commander of the Azad Hind Fauj was sown on that day.

At the Calcutta Congress, Gandhiji put forward the demand for dominion status for India—that is autonomy within the British Empire—within a year. But Bose and Nehru demanded complete independence.

The next couple of years saw Subhas Chandra more and more involved in political activity. He was very busy addressing youth meetings and political conferences. He particularly inspired the youth wherever he went.

In 1931, he was Mayor of Calcutta. On January 26th, 1931, the first Independence Day, he led a procession in the streets of Calcutta and was severely beaten up by the police.

In January 1932, started another prolonged imprisonment for Subhas. He was arrested on his way from Bombay to Calcutta. He had gone to meet Gandhiji in Bombay.

Once in jail his health broke down completely. He was shifted from one jail to another. He was kept at various sanatoriums and hospitals as prisoner for some time. Later, he was detained at Jabalpur prison along with his brother Sarat.

The British Government refused to release him though his health was completely ruined. At last the British Government proposed that they would put him on a ship for Europe and release him there.

So he was sent to forced exile in Europe. In February 1933, they put Subhas Chandra Bose on board S.S. 'Gange' bound for Italy.

Subhas Chandra Bose arrived in Vienna in the spring of 1933. He was given medical treatment. After a few weeks of treatment and rest he felt much better. As soon as he felt a little better he started to contact people all over Europe, people who belonged to different walks of life—academic, cultural or political. In those days, Europeans knew very little about India. They knew nothing of the sufferings of the Indian people under British rule or about India's struggle for freedom. The little news that reached them about India came through British sources; so very often they had a prejudiced version of Indian news.

Subhas Chandra Bose took upon himself the job of India's unofficial ambassador abroad. He decided to educate the people of Europe about India and to arouse their sympathy for the Nationalist Movement.

In Vienna he established the Austrian-Indian Society. He lectured and wrote about India. He made personal contacts with prominent people in the cultural and economic circles.

The British Government had tried to restrict his activities by giving him a passport valid only for Austria. But it was not so easy to hold back Subhas Chandra Bose. He contacted the consuls of Czechoslovakia and Poland and managed to obtain visas for visiting these countries. Even the British consul at Prague seemed to have been charmed by his personality and was quite helpful to Subhas although later he was taken to task by higher authorities.

In Czechoslovakia, Netaji formed the Czechoslovak-Indian Association together with Professor Lesny, a friend of Tagore. The Czech Foreign Minister, Dr. Benes, received him. The Czech people were very friendly towards India's freedom movement.

During World War I, Poland was under Russian domination. Polish people knew the humiliation of being a subject nation. They were also sympathetic to India's cause. Netaji came to know that during World War I, a Polish legion was trained in Japan to fight for the country's freedom.

From Poland he came to Germany and Italy. Hitler was all-in-all in Germany at that time. Nobody dared oppose him. But Subhas Chandra wanted to protest against the narrow racial policy followed by Hitier's regime. He wrote to official German newspapers protesting against racial discrimination.

Hitler had made some contemptuous remarks about Indians in his book *Mein Kampf*. Subhas tried to have a meeting with Hitler so that he might persuade him to correct those passages. But he was not allowed to meet Hitler.

In Italy, he met Mussolini. Mussolini was much impressed by the young Indian political leader. He asked him whether India's independence would be won by reformist or revolutionary methods. He was happy when Subhas Chandra said it was his belief that independence would come through revolutionary methods. Subhas Chandra Bose was also closely connected with the Indian Irish Independence League. Madame Macbride, a well-known Irish patriot, was the president of the league. Netaji met De Valera, leader of the Irish Independence movement, in Dublin and discussed with him many common problems which the two countries shared.

Subhas Chandra was interested in leaders like Hitler, Mussolini, De Valera or for that matter Kamal Ataturk of Turkey or Lenin and Stalin of Russia because he admired the way they had awakened the masses and organized them. Hitler and Mussolini had been condemned for their ideology. Netaji was not concerned with their internal policy. He wanted to find out the secret of the inspiration. The Indian masses must be mobilized for the final battle for freedom.

Subhas Chandra was not allowed to enter England for a very long time. He had been invited to preside over a political conference in London in 1933 but as he was not allowed to go to England he sent his address to be read in absentia. The British Government did not want him to come to London or to Berlin because there were large numbers of Indian students in these two cities. The Government feared Subhas Chandra

Bose's influence on them.

During his forced exile abroad he wrote his famous book, *The Indian Struggle*, in Vienna in 1934. The book was received well in Europe but was banned in India. In 1937, during a second visit to Badgastein in Austria, he wrote his unfinished autobiography, *An Indian Pilgrim*.

From 1933 onwards Subhas was almost continuously in Europe for three years. He lost his father in 1934. When he came to know of his critical condition he rushed home but reached too late to see him alive.

After the last rites were over he was sent back to Europe. But he was getting tired of his life in exile. In the beginning of 1936, Subhas Chandra defied government orders and came back to India. He wanted to attend the Lucknow Congress. But as soon as he set foot in Bombay he was promptly arrested. Nehru was presiding at the Lucknow Congress. Subhas Chandra could not come but he was made a member of the Working Committee. There was spontaneous protest all over the country against his arrest. An all-India hartal was also observed.

Imprisonment always ruined his health. In 1937, after his release, he spent a holiday at the hill resort of Dalhousie with his long-standing friends Dr. and Mrs. Dharmavir. In the winter of that year he again went to Badgastein for a short rest. Here, while writing *An Indian Pilgrim*, news reached him that he had been elected Rashtrapati or the President of the Indian Congress. It was a great honour in those days. En route to India he was allowed to enter Britain and stopped in London for a brief stay.

IV

RASHTRAPATI AND AFTER

On the eve of his forty-first birthday in January 1938 Subhas Chandra Bose arrived in India from Europe. He was now the Rashtrapati or the President of the Indian National Congress, one of the youngest Presidents so far. A very busy schedule awaited him.

The Congress session that year was held at a place called Haripura in Gujarat. It was the fifty-first annual gathering of the Congress. There was the usual pomp and grandeur. Fifty-one decorative gates were erected, fifty-one Congress flags were hoisted and the Rashtrapati drove in a chariot drawn by fifty-one bullocks.

The speech that Subhas Chandra Bose delivered as President of the Congress is a very important document in the history of our struggle for freedom. Some of the national problems which he discussed in his speech remain even to this day burning problems of free India.

Poverty is the main curse of India. So eradication of poverty would be our first task, he said. For this, on the one hand, we must rapidly build up new industry. This would help us to produce more and to provide employment for many. But on the other hand we must not forget that most of our population lived in the villages. Therefore, radical reform of the land system would be necessary. Our poor farmers must be given all help and encouragement.

Another problem of India is the question of language. There are a number of languages in India. Therefore, we needed a link language which would be accepted all over India. Subhas Chandra thought Hindustani written in Roman script, that is the English alphabet, would be the only practical solution. Every Indian knew some Hindustani and if it was written in the Roman script it would be easier for the non-Hindi speaking people. He had the opportunity to put this theory into practice when he recognized Hindustani in Roman script as the official language of the Provisional Government of Azad Hind in East Asia.

Nowadays we hear so much about the problem of our ever-growing population. Subhas Chandra was one of the first leaders to warn us about it. He said population must be checked otherwise all our good work would fall through.

Another topic that we hear being discussed a lot these days is planning. A country's economic development depends on good planning. As Congress President Subhas Chandra set up the first ever National Planning Committee. He asked Jawaharlal Nehru to be the chairman of the Committee. The poet Rabindranath Tagore showed keen interest in the planning of the country's economy. Others who helped were the noted scientist Meghnad Saha and the economist K.T. Shah.

The new Rashtrapati was very keen to find a solution to the vexed Hindu-Muslim question. He feared that if no solution was reached the country might ultimately be partitioned by the British imperialists. He met Mr. M.A. Jinnah, the Muslim League leader, several times. No solution, however, was possible because of Mr. Jinnah's rigid attitude. Later when Netaji created the Indian National Army he showed us how to achieve communal solidarity. Every soldier of the Indian National Army was an Indian first and then a Hindu, a Muslim or a Sikh.

Subhas Chandra Bose wanted to intensify international propaganda for Indian independence. We should accept the help of any nation whatever may be the internal political system of that country, he said. War would break out soon in Europe, he predicted. England would be busy defending itself. Subhas Bose saw no harm if India took advantage of England's difficulty.

At the end of his first term of presidentship, Subhas Chandra Bose decided to stand for election for a second term. The usual practice in those days was that the working committee under Gandhiji's direction decided who would be the president. The election itself was a mere formality. But that year the picture was different. Subhas Chandra's decision to stand for a second term was not liked by some of his colleagues including Gandhiji himself. Gandhiji nominated Pattabhi Sitaramayya.

A very painful phase of Indian politics followed. There were accusations and counter-accusations on both sides. Subhas Chandra said he wished to contest the elections not

because of

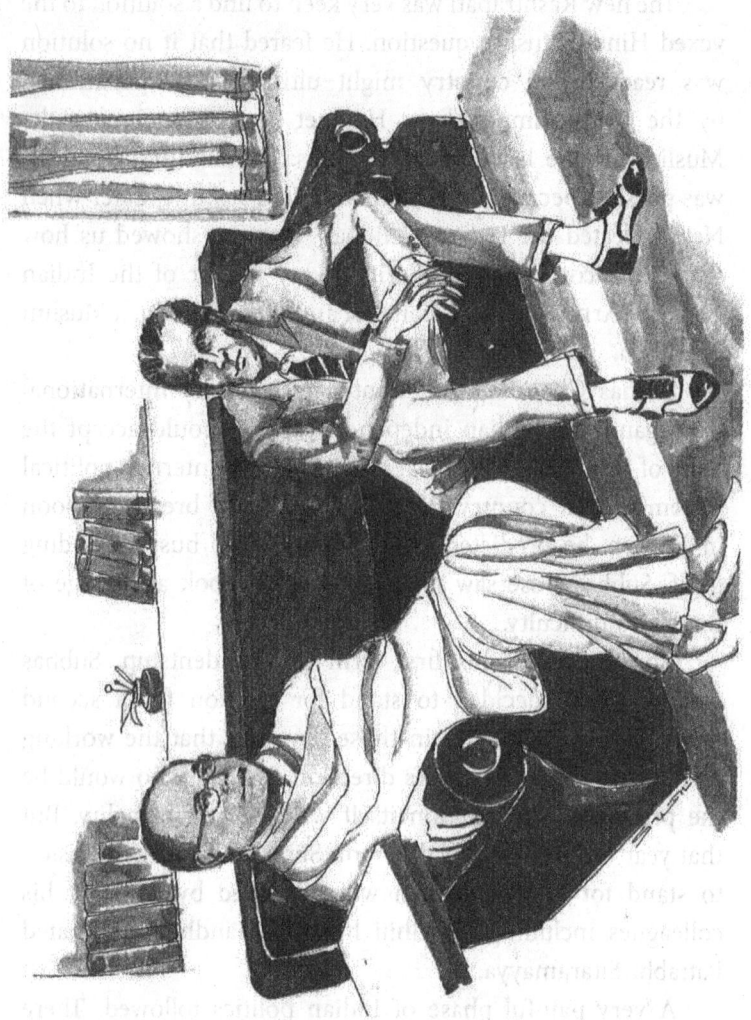

personal ambition but because he wanted to implement certain progressive plans and programmes which he had initiated. So unlike other years there was a keenly contested election.

Subhas Chandra Bose surprised his friends and foes alike by winning the election against bitter opposition from Gandhiji and his followers. Gandhiji was hurt and declared Pattabhi's defeat was his own defeat.

Subhas Chandra was deeply pained by Gandhiji's attitude. He tried his best to appease the Mahatma. He said: 'It will be a tragic thing for me if I succeed in winning the confidence of other people but fail to win the confidence of India's greatest man.'

The next Congress session took place in Tripuri in Madhya Pradesh. Subhas Chandra Bose fell seriously ill on the eve of the session. The Rashtrapati was carried on a stretcher. He was running a high temperature and was unable to read his presidential address himself. The Mahatma refused to come to Tripuri. And his followers refused to cooperate with the new president.

In his short Presidential speech, which was read out by his brother Sarat, he said we must give an ultimatum to the British Government to grant us freedom. It was March 1939. The clouds of war had already gathered over Europe. Subhas Chandra thought, the international situation was ripe for a final assault on the British Empire. The enemy's difficulty would be India's opportunity.

But the other leaders were not in a mood to listen to him. Even after Tripuri, the Bose-Gandhi differences dragged on for some time. The poet Rabindranath Tagore interceded on Subhas Chandra's behalf. He appealed to Gandhiji to apply his healing touch to wounded feelings. Pandit Nehru, though opposed to Subhas in this contest, tried for a settlement. He wrote to Gandhiji that Subhas was susceptible to a friendly approach and if Gandhiji met him a settlement might be possible.

But nothing could prevent the final parting of ways. Subhas Chandra Bose resigned from the presidency at an All India Congress Committee meeting held in Calcutta in April, 1939.

But whatever happened between Gandhiji and Subhas Chandra their mutual regard and affection were not permanently impaired. In his last meeting with Subhas in June 1940, Gandhiji told him that he did not think the time was opportune for a final struggle. But if Subhas thought otherwise he should go ahead. 'If you come out successful I shall be the first to congratulate you,' said the Mahatma. On the other hand, it was Netaji who first called Gandhiji 'Father of our Nation'. When Netaji led the Indian National Army in battle, in a radio broadcast addressed to Gandhiji he said—'Father of our Nation! In this holy war for India's liberation we ask for your blessings and good wishes.'

Subhas Chandra Bose's eleventh and last imprisonment started on July 3rd, 1940. The past year had been hectic for him. He had formed the Forward Bloc. Initially it was to work within the Congress but it soon became a separate body. When the Congress session was held at Ramgarh, Subhas Chandra organized by its side another conference known as the Anti-Compromise Conference. Later that year he held another national conference in Nagpur. At that time World War II was raging in Europe. Britain was in great trouble.

'All power to the Indian people here and now'—was the

slogan that Subhas Chandra Bose raised.

Subhas's last imprisonment was, however, short. At Calcutta's Presidency Jail, Subhas felt restless. The war had brought a great opportunity for India. Britain was fighting for its own survival. But here he was languishing in prison and unable to seize the opportunity.

So he declared a fast unto death demanding release. And when his condition became serious he was released from prison on December 5th, 1940.

The British Government did not wish to take the risk of his death in prison but decided they would rearrest him when he was a little better. They would play cat and mouse with him.

But that was not to be. Subhas Chandra Bose had his own plans. On the night of 16th-17th January he escaped from his Elgin Road house in the guise of Mohammad Ziauddin. For ten days the news of his escape was a closely guarded secret. It had been announced—earlier, that Subhas Chandra was living in seclusion in order to observe certain religious rites.

After ten days his elder brother Sarat Chandra made a plan of how the news of his escape should be made public. Instead of the police first discovering it, the news was to be divulged in a normal manner.

Having made the plans Sarat Chandra Bose left with his family for his country house in Rishra near Calcutta. Every day a plate of food was placed in Subhas Chandra's room and someone ate the food and then pushed the plate out. On that day, the food remained untouched according to plan. The cook was genuinely worried and raised an alarm. Most of the family, including Subhas's old mother, knew nothing about the escape. So the alarm was, indeed, genuine. A few who knew pretended to raise a hue and cry. Some left for Rishra to 'inform' Sarat Bose who rushed back to Calcutta.

A search was carried out in temples and monasteries in and around Calcutta. It was generally believed that he must have renounced the material world and gone to the Himalayas. The notorious British Intelligence was for once totally baffled.

Anxious enquiries poured in from all over India. Gandhiji cabled, 'Please, wire truth'. It was not possible to do so. Sarat Bose cabled back, 'Circumstances indicate renunciation'. In answer to Rabindranath Tagore's message, he wrote, 'Hope he will have your blessings wherever he may be.'

When all this was going on in Calcutta, Subhas Chandra Bose crossed the frontier safely and entered Afghanistan. And after a prolonged stay in Kabul finally left for Berlin in the guise of an Italian named Orlando Mazzotta.

V
AZAD HIND

Subhas Chandra Bose in the disguise of Orlando Mazzotta arrived in Berlin in the first week of April, 1941. He was a man who could never sit idle. Every minute of his life he must spend on his life's mission fighting for India's liberation. Within a few days of his arrival in Berlin he submitted a document to the German Foreign Minister, Ribbentrop, in which he outlined in detail his future policy and programme.

He planned to establish a Free India Centre in Berlin. From this centre he would organize an Indian National Army. The army would be recruited from the men of the British Indian Army who had been taken prisoner by the Germans and Italians. Netaji also wanted to carry on anti-British propaganda through radio broadcasts. For all this he needed the help of the German Government.

Many people ask why Netaji chose to go to Germany

during the war. He did so because Germany was fighting Great Britain. Netaji believed we would be justified in taking the help of the enemy's enemy. We, the Indian people, have been fighting the British Imperialists for a long time. But we were an unarmed people. It was Netaji's belief that in the final phase of our struggle for freedom an armed struggle would be necessary. World War II opened up great opportunities for India in this respect. Netaji knew Hitler's narrow, racist views and the nature of Nazi Germany. When he was in Europe in the 30s he had closely watched Nazi Germany. He had no illusions about it. Still he decided to take the plunge.

Fortunately for Netaji there were some sincere friends of India at the Special India Division of the German Foreign Office. Adam Von Trott was in charge of the desk. He was the man who was later convicted in the plot to assassinate Hitler and hanged. However, at that time Trott was very much in command of the desk. His deputy was Alexander Werth, another great friend of India. Wilhelm Keppler was the Secretary of State who maintained the link between the central government machinery and the India Division.

Soon with the cooperation of the Special India Division, Netaji was able to set up the Free India Centre in Berlin. Its office was on Liechtensteinalle and Netaji was given a villa on Sophienstrasse. The Free India Centre was granted the status of a diplomatic mission. For organizing the centre Netaji took loans from the German Government, to be repaid when India became free. But even before India was free, Netaji started repaying the loan. When the Provisional Government of Azad Hind was established in Singapore and the Government had funds of its own from donations of Indians in South East Asia,

Netaji repaid several million yen to the German Government.

The Free India Centre was soon bristling with activity. The Azad Hind Radio started functioning with a team of young Indians. Netaji went round the camps where soldiers of the British Indian Army were imprisoned. Inspired by Netaji, many of them decided to fight for their country's freedom. An Indian legion consisting of these recruits was trained by German military experts. Many other civilian Indians residing in Germany or for that matter in other parts of Europe joined the Free India Centre. Among them were A.C.N. Nambiar, Abid Hasan, N.G. Swami, M.R. Vyas, N.G. Ganpuley, Girija Mukherji, J.K. Banerji and many others.

It was a period of hectic but long-term planning. Many of the plans chalked out in Germany were actually put into practice later in Singapore and Burma. *Jana Gana Mana* was chosen as the national anthem. It was the Free India Centre in Germany that introduced 'Jai Hind' as the common greeting for all Indians. Hindustani in Roman script was adopted as the official language. It was also in Germany that people started calling Subhas Chandra Bose—'Netaji' as a mark of honour and affection. The Centre published its official journal *Azad Hind* which was circulated throughout Europe. Free India stamps were printed for use in liberated India.

Great stress was laid on communal harmony. Everyone was Indian first and Indian last fighting for the liberation of India. It did not matter whether a person was a Hindu or a Muslim, a Punjabi or a Bengali or a Sikh. Everyone, however, had the right to worship in his own way. It was a personal matter. It is interesting, however, that Netaji disapproved of common prayers. Once the Indian legion soldiers wrote a common prayer addressed neither to Rama nor to Rahim but to Malik, the Urdu word for the Lord. But Netaji disapproved of it because it was his view that it was dangerous to ask people to unite in the name of religion. In that case it also became easy to divide them in the name of religion. Religion and politics, in Netaji's opinion, must be completely divorced from each other.

The British divided the Indian army into various community and religious groups like the Rajput, the Dogra, the Punjabi, etc. But in Netaji's Indian National Army different communities were mixed up in each regiment. Food was cooked and served in the same kitchen to be shared by all. Netaji was a man of uncompromisingly independent spirit. Although he was organizing the liberation movement of his own country in a foreign land ruled by a dictator he would not bow his head to anyone. The broadcasts of the Azad Hind Radio were not to be censored by the German Government. Netaji also made it an unalterable condition that the I.N.A. would not be used against any nation other than the British. In international policy matters, Netaji also followed an independent line. For example, when Germany attacked Soviet Russia, Netaji told the Nazi regime clearly that he disapproved of it and that Germany would be looked upon by Indians as the aggressor.

Netaji had been demanding from the German Government a formal declaration guaranteeing India's freedom but Hitler, for his own reasons, did not agree to publicly issue such a declaration. Netaji had only one meeting with Hitler in May 1942. But nothing much came of it. On the other hand, Hitler's armies were bogged down in the vast plains of Russia.

In the meantime, Japan had declared war on the

Anglo-Americans in December 1941 and was marching ahead. It occupied Burma and reached the doorstep of India. Netaji thought he would be able to serve India much better if he could go over to Japan and lead a liberation army from the East. Hitler agreed to help him in this undertaking and a journey under the sea in a submarine was arranged.

Netaji left behind the Free India Centre and the Indian Legion to be looked after by A.C.N. Nambiar. He also left behind his wife Emilie and his three-month-old daughter Anita. Emilie and Netaji had known each other in Vienna since 1934. When Netaji wrote his book on the Indian struggle for freedom she had worked with him closely. She had also come to be deeply involved in the work of India's freedom movement abroad. When Netaji arrived in Berlin during the war, Emilie was the first to be called from Vienna. She joined her husband in his grand task.

On February 8th, 1943, Netaji left Germany in a submarine from the port of Kiel. In a letter dated February 8th, he wrote to his elder brother Sarat:

> Today I am again starting on a voyage of danger... I do not know if I shall see the end of the voyage. In case we do not meet any more in this life...

But Netaji did see the end of this voyage. And after a perilous journey reached Tokyo ninety days later. There began the final and the most fascinating phase of his life.

VI

A PERILOUS JOURNEY

Netaji's historic escape from India, his dangerous journey from Calcutta to Berlin via Kabul has become legendary. But Netaji undertook another perilous journey in February 1943 which brought him from Berlin to Tokyo. This time it was a journey by submarine that lasted ninety days and at a time when the whole world was plunged in a deadly war.

Netaji left Berlin by train from the Lehrterbanhoffe for Kiel. He was seen off at Kiel by State Secretary Keppler, Alexander Werth and A.C.N. Nambiar. When Netaji and his secretary Abid Hasan boarded the submarine they were welcomed by Werner Musemberg, the captain of the boat. Netaji's departure was absolutely a closely guarded secret. Even Abid Hasan was not told where exactly they were going until they had left Berlin.

The German and the Japanese Navy had worked out the plan very carefully and this took quite a long time. In fact, Netaji was getting very impatient because of the delay. Eventually General Oshima, the Japanese Ambassador in Berlin, informed him in January 1943 that plans were ready. The Japanese Navy had stated the exact position in the Indian Ocean where a Japanese submarine would pick Netaji up from the German submarine.

Life in the submarine was naturally cramped and restricted. Even so, Netaji kept himself fully occupied. During this journey he was chalking out future plans for the struggle in East Asia. He dictated long speeches to Abid Hasan, speeches he would deliver in Tokyo and Singapore. But in actual fact Netaji never read from a prepared speech. He always preferred to speak extempore. So when points were discussed and notes typed, he glanced over them once or twice and then tore them up. Abid Hasan's heart used to bleed. Why then this futile exercise, he thought. But it was not futile. Netaji meant to do his home work well and was always prepared.

One day, Netaji was dictating to Abid Hasan a speech which he planned to address to the womenfolk of East Asia asking them to organize an army of their own to be called the Rani of Jhansi Regiment. Just at that time the submarine was suddenly faced with grave danger. It had surfaced by mistake and was spotted by a British freighter. The freighter came charging at full speed and brushed against the railing of the submarine which had just managed to duck. But the impact threw it on one side and everything was topsy-turvy. In the midst of general confusion and panic, Abid Hasan heard the calm voice of Netaji—'Hasan, I have dictated a line twice but you have not taken it down.'

'Sorry, Sir,' he replied and with trembling fingers started taking notes again.

When the commotion subsided the captain of the submarine told the crew that they must all take a lesson as to how to remain calm in the face of crisis from the distinguished Indian guest and his adjutant.

The submarine sailed down the Atlantic Ocean along the coast of West Africa to the Indian Ocean. When the submarine surfaced at night from time to time, Netaji came up and sat on the deck and chatted with Abid Hasan. Abid Hasan, apart from being his secretary, occasionally also cooked for Netaji and prepared 'khichri' for him. At the dining table, Netaji offered it to German officers and crew. As they were passing the French coast, another German boat brought supplies to them for the long and arduous voyage ahead.

At long last they reached the point of rendezvous to the south of Madagascar. There the Japanese submarine appeared. It was a very difficult manoeuvre, transhipment of passengers from one submarine to another. To make things worse the weather was bad and the sea extremely rough. The two submarines had sighted each other on the night of April 26th, 1943. But they could not pose side by side for the transhipment. A whole day was spent in futile attempts at transhipment. In desperation two German sailors jumped into the dangerously rough sea in the evening and swam to the Japanese boat. The Japanese were shocked at the risk the Germans took. They held a joint conference to decide what should be done. Next morning, the seas still continued to be rough. The two Germans in the Japanese submarine rode back to their own boat in a rubber dinghy and dragged a very strong rope along with them after fastening it securely to the Japanese boat.

Netaji bade goodbye to the German crew and got into the rubber dinghy. Abid Hasan followed him. The rubber dinghy swayed dangerously in the water and both passengers were drenched. The rope was pulled slowly towards the Japanese submarine. As Netaji climbed into the Japanese submarine Commander Izu and Captain Terauka welcomed him. The Japanese boat was bigger and more comfortable. The kitchen had some ingredients for Indian cooking picked up from Penang—for the distinguished passenger. On the 29th of April there was a big celebration in the submarine on the occasion of the Japanese Emperor's birthday. Netaji joined the celebrations.

The Japanese submarine took them to Sabang, a small islet off the coast of Sumatra. Netaji posed for a photograph with the crew and then shook hands with each and every one of them as he said goodbye. For Commander Izu and most of the officers it was a final parting with Netaji. Because soon thereafter, Commander Izu and others were killed during another voyage.

At Sabang, Netaji was welcomed by Bin Yamamoto, an old friend whom he had known as the Military Attache at the Japanese Embassy in Berlin. Yamamoto was now head of the Hikari Kikan, an organization which was to act as liaison agency between the Azad Hind Government and the Japanese Government.

After resting for a few days, Netaji flew to Tokyo on May 16th, 1943.

VII

ON TO DELHI

From Calcutta to Kabul, Netaji was Mohammad Ziauddin. From Kabul to Berlin, Netaji was Orlando Mazzotta. When he arrived in Tokyo on May 16th, 1943, he was supposed to be a Japanese named Matsuda.

For the next three weeks Netaji was extremely busy. He met the Japanese Foreign Minister, Shigemitsu, the Chief of Navy Sugiyama and other top officials of the Japanese Foreign Office. The Japanese did not, naturally, know much about the Indian political situation. Netaji narrated to them the long history of India's struggle for independence. The officials found the background information most useful. On the other hand, they introduced Netaji to various Japanese institutions. He was taken round Tokyo and shown factories and shipyards, schools and universities.

Before he met Netaji, Japanese Prime Minister Tojo was not

very enthusiastic about the question of India's independence. He had reasons to be cool. About a year before Netaji's arrival in South East Asia an Indian National Army had been formed in Singapore by Captain Mohan Singh from amongst the prisoners of war of the British Indian Army. Captain Mohan Singh himself was of the same army. But the Japanese authorities and the Indian National Army did not get on well. So the army was disbanded.

But when he met Netaji in Tokyo, Tojo was absolutely charmed by his personality. A few days later, Tojo made a historic declaration in the Japanese Parliament assuring all support to Indian Freedom Movement.

After this Netaji held a Press conference and he revealed to the world his presence in Japan and expressed his determination of fighting the last final battle with the British. 'The enemy has drawn the sword and he must be fought with the sword,' he declared.

Netaji arrived in Singapore accompanied by the veteran revolutionary leader Rashbehari Bose who had been a long-time exile in Japan. There were a large number of Indians in Singapore and also a large number of Indian prisoners of war there who had joined the Indian National Army. At a historic meeting on July 4th, 1943, Rashbehari Bose announced that from that day onwards Subhas Chandra Bose would be the leader of the Indian Independence Movement. Netaji made a passionate speech in reply. He called upon the Indians in East Asia to pay the price for freedom by shedding their blood and giving up their all for the cause.

On July 5th, 1943, in Singapore's main city square thirteen thousand soldiers of the Indian National Army lined up and listened to Netaji spellbound. After reviewing the army he said:

> Soldiers of India's Army of Liberation, today is the proudest day of my life. Today it has pleased Providence to give me the unique privilege and honour of announcing to the whole world that India's Army of Liberation has come into being.

All the soldiers were deeply moved when Netaji called upon them to sacrifice their all and said: 'For the present I can offer you nothing except hunger, thirst, privation, forced marches and death. But if you follow me in life and in death as I am confident you will, I shall lead you to victory and freedom.'

There were wild scenes of enthusiasm wherever Netaji went. Womenfolk came up and gave their ornaments for the war chest. Rich businessmen donated their all in the service of the Azad Hind Movement. Here was a leader for whom they were prepared to sacrifice everything.

Netaji was a superb organizer. He turned all the enthusiasm and emotion into a well-organized movement. The Provisional Government of Azad Hind was formed on October 21st, 1943. Netaji was the Head of State and Prime Minister of the newly-formed Government and also the Supreme Commander of the Army. Among the other Ministers were S.A. Ayer who was in charge of propaganda and publicity and A.C. Chatterji in charge of finance. The only woman member of the Cabinet was Capt. Lakshmi Swaminathan who was Minister-in-Charge of Women's Organization.

It was a War Cabinet. So there were a number of army officers in it. Netaji was fortunate in having a number of loyal and efficient officers. Among them were Major-General Bhonsle, Major-General M.Z. Kiani, Colonel Gulzara Singh, Colonel Habibur Rahaman, Colonel Inayet Kiani, Major Abid Hasan, not to speak of Major-General Shah Nawaz Khan, Colonel P.K. Sahgal and Colonel Dhillon who were later tried in the Red Fort. The different brigades of the army were named Gandhi Brigade, Nehru Brigade, Azad Brigade (named after Maulana Azad, the then President of the Congress) and Subhas Brigade.

The I.N.A. had a women's wing, the Rani of Jhansi Regiment. Women fought side by side with the menfolk and distinguished themselves. The children felt left out. Why could not they also do something for their motherland? So children between the ages of nine and fourteen were organized into a group called Bal Sena. Although they were not sent to the front they were of great help in many other ways when their elders were fighting away from home. A group of forty-five young boys were sent by Netaji to the Tokyo Military Academy for military training. They were known as the Tokyo Cadets to whom Netaji was very attached.

When we peep into Netaji's household we see so many interesting scenes and situations. We find him sometimes at the dining table sharing a simple meal with his officers. He would be cracking jokes with the table boy Kali. As he enjoyed the dahi and banana he would say—'Bananas are expensive, Kali, what shall we eat tomorrow?' He would sometimes crack a joke at his own expense. He told the officers over dinner one day that when he had undertaken a fast unto death in Calcutta's Presidency Jail the Superintendent tried to dissuade him. He told Netaji, 'Look here, Mr. Bose, a live donkey is better than a dead lion.' Netaji burst into laughter as he told them the story.

There were a number of pets in Netaji's household, monkeys, goats, rabbits. The two monkeys were Ramu and Sita. Ramu used to jump on Netaji's shoulder and pull at the few strands of hair on his head. Then he would take a banana from Netaji's hands and jump off again. Netaji did not like cats but as his Private Secretary Abid Hasan was fond of them and secretly brought in kittens into the house, Netaji had to put up with them too.

In the meantime, war preparations were going on. Netaji attended a very important conference in Tokyo in November 1943. It was the Greater East Asia Conference. At this conference, Tojo declared that the Andaman and Nicobar Islands would be transferred to the Provisional Government of Azad Hind. Andaman and Nicobar thus became the first independent Indian territory. An Indian governor was appointed. Netaji later paid a visit to the islands and renamed them Shaheed and Swaraj.

The seat of the Azad Hind Government was moved from Singapore to Rangoon in 1944. The Azad Hind Fauj marched to the borders of India. 'Chalo Delhi' was their war cry. On March 18th, they crossed the Indo-Burma frontier and stood on Indian soil. There was great jubilation all around. Kohima was captured on the 6th of April after bitter fighting.

The I.N.A. moved into Manipur. There was fierce fighting in and around Bishenpur. Then on April 4th, Col. Shaukat Malik of the Bahadur group of the I.N.A. unfurled the tricolour of India at Moirang, a place only twelve miles away from Imphal.

The Imphal operation, however, ended tragically for the I.N.A. The Anglo-American armies were reinforced by air. The I.N.A. had no air support and their long communication lines broke down completely. To make matters worse the monsoon came early that year. The I.N.A. had to beat a retreat.

The retreat itself was disastrous. Thousands of people died of starvation and disease. But the spirit of the I.N.A. was indomitable. Did not Netaji give them the warning that there would be hunger, thirst, privation, forced marches and death?

The I.N.A. fought fearlessly as their Supreme Commander was the personification of fearlessness. Once Netaji was reviewing a march-past by the I.N.A. near Rangoon when the British mounted an air attack. He continued to stand at the saluting base while bombs were falling all around him till the last soldier had marched past. He left the platform and took shelter only after all the rest had done so.

When the battered army reached Moulmein, Netaji came to visit the army. Netaji met each officer individually and embraced him. His mere presence had a healing touch.

An I.N.A. officer who was later arrested by the British was asked at the time of his interrogation why he followed Netaji in spite of all the misery and suffering. 'What did you get in return?' he was asked. The officer replied calmly, 'Netaji embraced me once.'

When Rangoon was about to fall to the British, Netaji was asked to leave Rangoon. The Japanese offered him transport. But Netaji refused to leave Rangoon until arrangements were made for the evacuation of his army, particularly the girls of the Rani of Jhansi Regiment. So alternative arrangements were made and the retreat from Rangoon started on April 24th, 1945.

This was a historic retreat. Netaji shared with his men and women all the hardships of a long trek on foot across a most difficult terrain. The cars and trucks were soon destroyed. They walked during the night and took shelter in villages during the day. Enemy bombers harassed them all the time. But nothing could crush the spirit of the soldiers. The girls of the Rani of Jhansi Regiment laughed and joked as they cooked improvised meals at the roadside. The presence of Netaji gave them limitless inspiration. Many of the soldiers later recalled the retreat as one of the greatest experiences of their lives.

In the meantime, the war situation had changed for the worse for Japan. On August 6th, the atom bomb was dropped on Hiroshima. Japan surrendered to the Allies on August 15th, 1945.

At Singapore, Netaji conferred with his cabinet colleagues and military officers. He treated the defeat as a temporary setback. A revolutionary war never comes to an end. In a message to his followers Netaji said:

> In this unprecedented crisis in our history, I have only one word to say. Do not be depressed at our temporary failure. Be of good cheer and keep up your spirits. Above all never for a moment falter in your faith in India's destiny. There is no power on earth that can keep India enslaved. India shall be free and before long.

The date of the message is August 15th, 1945. In exactly two years his words came true.

VIII

VICTORY IN DEFEAT

It is however an irony of history that the apparent defeat of the Indian National Army turned into a permanent victory for the Indian people. We do not know of any other instance where a defeated army has done so much for the freedom of its motherland.

At the end of the war, a large number of I.N.A. officers and men were arrested by the British. Three of the officers were brought to Delhi for trial. The trial was held at the famous Red Fort of Delhi. When Netaji gave the call 'On to Delhi'—'Chalo Delhi', he had declared that the I.N.A. would one day march to Delhi and hold its victory parade at the ancient Red Fortress of India's metropolis. Now, officers were there not at the head of a victorious army but as prisoners of war. Of the three, Major-General Shah Nawaz Khan was a Muslim, Colonel P.K. Sahgal, a Hindu and Colonel Dhillon, a Sikh.

Unwittingly the British brought to the fore the representative character of the Indian National Army. The news of their arrest and trial enraged the people of India.

The Red Fort trial was a blunder on the part of the British Government. During the war not many people inside India knew about the exploits of the I.N.A. The Azad Hind Radio broadcasts did not reach all parts of the vast country or the masses of our people. The limited few who tuned in to such broadcasts had to do so secretly for fear of detection and punishment by the police. The Red Fort trial, however, brought the whole story to light. The people of India were thrilled to know that a Provisional Government of Azad Hind had been formed by Netaji Subhas Chandra Bose and that an Army of Liberation had marched up to Manipur.

At the end of World War II, the freedom struggle inside India was at its lowest ebb. The nationalist leaders were all thrown into prison during the Quit India Movement of 1942 which was ruthlessly crushed by the ruling power. The leaders came out of prison weary in body and spirit. The people generally were demoralized. All of a sudden the heroic saga of the I.N.A. electrified India from one end to the other.

All over India there was mass agitation demanding the release of the I.N.A. officers. Almost all political parties were united on this issue. The Congress formed a Defence Committee for the I.N.A. Bhulabhai Desai was the Chief Counsel. Even Jawaharlal Nehru put on his barrister's gown once again and appeared for the defence.

There was an unprecedented emotional upsurge throughout the length and breadth of the country. At first the government tried to put the movement down by force. The police even

resorted to large-scale firing all over the country. Many people were killed. But gradually the British Government came to realize that it would no longer be possible to rule India with the help of the British Indian Army. The popular upsurge for the I.N.A. had shaken the loyalty of the British Indian Army and aroused their national consciousness. In Bombay and other places a mutiny broke out in the Indian Navy. Serious trouble also broke out in the ranks of the army and the air force.

So the British decided to transfer power to the Indians. But before leaving India they struck a severe blow to Nationalist India by partitioning the country into two. If Netaji was present he would never have agreed to the division of the motherland on religious grounds. But unfortunately for India, at a most critical moment of our history, Netaji was not there to guide the nation.

To go back to our narrative in South East Asia, Netaji left Singapore on August 15th, 1945. The previous night the girls of the Rani of Jhansi Regiment had organized a show for I.N.A. officers and men. They staged a drama on the heroic life of Lakshmibai, the Rani of Jhansi who had fought the British way back in 1857 during the Sepoy Mutiny. They had invited Netaji to the show.

Netaji was at that time in the midst of a non-stop Cabinet meeting. Important last-minute decisions had to be taken. Even so he came to the show although a little late. The girls of the Rani of Jhansi Regiment put up a superb performance. As Netaji watched the drama, I.N.A. officers whispered important messages into his ears from time to time. At the end of the show, about three thousand I.N.A. officers and men stood up and sang the national anthem.

It would have been wonderful if our story could have ended here with the patriotic soldiers singing the national anthem with Netaji in their midst. But real life is never like a fairy tale where everyone lives happily ever after.

Netaji left Singapore and halted in Bangkok for a day. He flew to Saigon on August 17th. The last available photograph of Netaji was taken when he was coming down the steps of the aircraft at Saigon airport.

The same day in the afternoon Netaji, accompanied by Colonel Habib-ur-Rahaman, left Saigon in another plane. He said Jai Hind to five of his ministers and army officers who saw him off at the airport. They were to follow him the next day after necessary arrangements for their journey had been made.

It is believed Netaji was going to Manchuria to seek asylum in Soviet Russia. He had decided to continue the war of independence from some other territory.

But destiny ordained otherwise. Netaji's plane landed in Taipei in Formosa for refuelling on August 18th, 1945. It was reported that while taking off the plane crashed. Among those who were killed instantly was a top Japanese military officer, General Shidei, who was going to take charge of the Japanese forces in Manchuria. It was further reported that Netaji was severely burnt and injured. He, along with the others, was rushed to the military hospital at Taipei. It was announced by Japanese Military Headquarters five days later that Netaji died the same evening.

Netaji told Habib-ur-Rahaman who was also injured but not so seriously: *Jab apney mulk wapis jayen to mulk ki bhaiyon ko batana ki men akhri dam tak mulk ki azadi key liyay larta raha hoon; woh jange Azadi ko jari rakhen. Hindustan zaroor azad hoga, us ko koi gulam nahin rakh sakta.*' ('When you go back to the motherland, tell my countrymen that I have been fighting for the liberation of my country till the last breath of my life; they must continue the struggle, India shall be free and before long. No power can keep India enslaved any longer.')

Many people in India, however, find it hard to believe that he is no more. The man who could fool British Intelligence and escape from Calcutta to Berlin, the man who could travel all the way from Germany to Japan in a submarine in the thick of a world war surely had a charmed life!

Long ago in the course of a benediction, Rabindranath Tagore had said of Netaji: 'I can only bless him and take my leave knowing that he has made his country's burden of sorrow his own, that his final reward is fast coming as his country's freedom.' Freedom came.

Now it remains for the new generation in India to rebuild their country in accordance with ideas and principles that Netaji has left behind. It was Netaji's belief: 'In this mortal world everything perishes and will perish—but ideas, ideals and dreams do not...the ideas, ideals and dreams of one generation are bequeathed to the next.'